EARTHQUAKES

Paul Mason

A+

Smart Apple Media
P.O. Box 3263
Mankato, MN, 56002

First published in 2011 by
MACMILLAN EDUCATION AUSTRALIA PTY LTD
15–19 Claremont St, South Yarra, Australia 3141

Visit our web site at www.macmillan.com.au or go directly to www.macmillanlibrary.com.au

Associated companies and representatives throughout the world.

Library of Congress Cataloging-in-Publication Data has been applied for.

Publisher: Carmel Heron
Commissioning Editor: Niki Horin
Managing Editor: Vanessa Lanaway
Editors: Philip Bryan and Tim Clarke
Proofreader: Kylie Cockle
Designer: Cristina Neri, Canary Graphic Design
Page layout: Cristina Neri, Canary Graphic Design
Photo researcher: Jes Senbergs (management: Debbie Gallagher)
Illustrator: Peter Bull Art Studio
Production Controller: Vanessa Johnson

Manufactured in China by Macmillan Production (Asia) Ltd.
Kwun Tong, Kowloon, Hong Kong
Supplier Code: CP January 2011

Acknowledgments
The Publisher would like to thank the Victoria State Emergency Service for their assistance in reviewing
these manuscripts.

The author and publisher are grateful to the following for permission to reproduce copyright material:

Front cover photograph: A picture shows the wrecked facade of the Westende Jewellers and rubble
blocking a street after a powerful 7.0 earthquake in Christchurch on September 4, 2010, courtesy Getty
Images/AFP.

Photographs courtesy of: Corbis, **12**, /Sergio Dorantes, **10**, /Dweitt Jones, **8**, /Roger Ressmeyer, **17**, /Patrick
Robert, **4**; Getty Images/AFP, **21**, **23**, **26**, **27**, **28**, /ChinaFotoPress, **15**; iStockPhoto/Matt Matthews, **18**, /Dan
Moore, **5**, /Julia Nichols, **24**; MSF/Kadir van Lohuizen/NOOR, **7**; Photolibrary/Hiromi Morita, **19**; Reuters/
Crack Palinggi, **11**; Shutterstock/Henrik Wither Andersen, **22**, /Machkazu, **20** (right), /Jenny Solomon, **16**, /
Jack Z. Young, **25**; UN Photo/Mark Garten, **29**; Wikipedia, **13**, **20** (left).

CONTENTS

DISASTER WORDS

When a word is printed in **bold**, look for its meaning in the "Disaster Words" box.

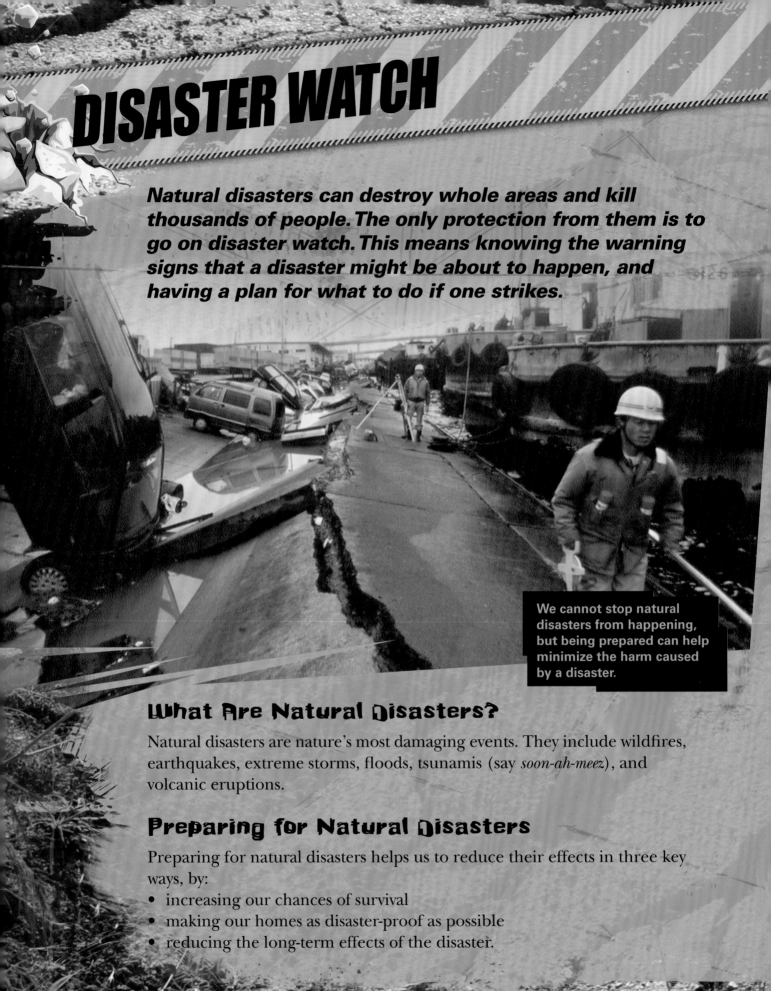

DISASTER WATCH

Natural disasters can destroy whole areas and kill thousands of people. The only protection from them is to go on disaster watch. This means knowing the warning signs that a disaster might be about to happen, and having a plan for what to do if one strikes.

We cannot stop natural disasters from happening, but being prepared can help minimize the harm caused by a disaster.

What Are Natural Disasters?

Natural disasters are nature's most damaging events. They include wildfires, earthquakes, extreme storms, floods, tsunamis (say *soon-ah-meez*), and volcanic eruptions.

Preparing for Natural Disasters

Preparing for natural disasters helps us to reduce their effects in three key ways, by:
- increasing our chances of survival
- making our homes as disaster-proof as possible
- reducing the long-term effects of the disaster.

EARTHQUAKES

Earthquakes can shake apart buildings and structures, causing death and injury. Millions of people live in areas threatened by earthquakes, so they need to know what to do if an earthquake strikes.

What Is an Earthquake?

An earthquake is the movement of the sheets of rock below Earth's surface. This movement makes the ground shake from side to side and up and down.

Preparing for an Earthquake

There are three key ways to prepare for an earthquake. You must know:

- the warning signs that a dangerous earthquake is on its way
- the safest places to be during an earthquake, and how to reach them
- the challenges facing those who survive an earthquake.

In 2010, a powerful earthquake hit Haiti, in the Caribbean. Around 300 000 people died and millions of people were left without homes, food or drinking water.

EYEWITNESS WORDS

Robert Bucari witnessed a major earthquake hit Alaska, United States, in 1964:

"I saw the parking lot moving in waves that looked like waves on an ocean. The walls of the [gym] next door were moving back and forth as if they were made of rubber."

Earthquakes happen all the time, all around the world. However, the most violent earthquakes are more likely to strike in certain areas. In particular, countries around the edges of the Pacific Ocean are regularly hit by powerful earthquakes.

Earthquakes Happen Everywhere

There are earthquakes happening in almost every country all the time. There are millions of earthquakes every year – Southern California alone has roughly 10,000 earthquakes each year! However, most earthquakes are so small that only the most sensitive measuring equipment can detect them.

This map shows where earthquakes happened between 1900 and 2000.

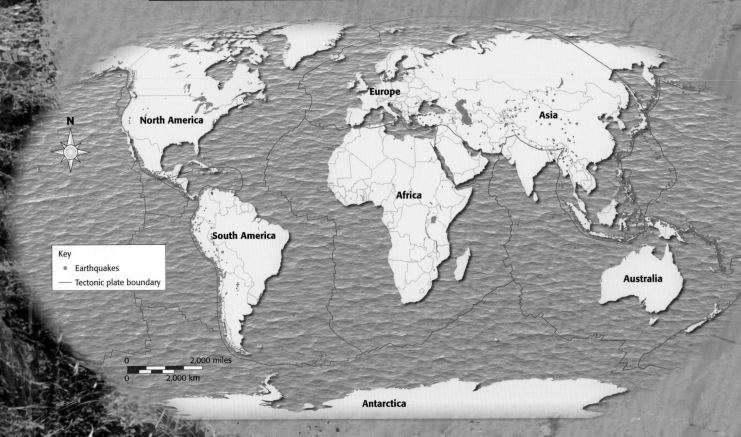

N

North America

Europe

Asia

Africa

South America

Australia

Antarctica

Key
- • Earthquakes
- — Tectonic plate boundary

0 — 2,000 miles

0 — 2,000 km

Areas Most Affected by Earthquakes

Powerful earthquakes are most common in mountainous regions, and around the edges of the Pacific Ocean, in an area called the Pacific Rim.

The Pacific Rim

The land around the Pacific Rim contains a large number of volcanoes. Earthquakes and volcanoes usually happen in the same areas, and violent earthquakes are regular events in many countries around the Pacific Rim.

Mountainous Areas

Extreme earthquakes are also common in mountainous regions. Major earthquakes have affected mountainous regions of Asia, the Middle East, and Southern Europe.

Where Earthquakes Do the Most Damage

Earthquakes cause the most damage in places that are densely populated. People living in cities around the Pacific Rim, such as San Francisco, United States, and Tokyo, Japan, are constantly alert for any signs of an earthquake.

The 2010 Haitian Earthquake

Magnitude: 7.0
Date: January 12, 2010
Location: Port-au-Prince, Haiti

The 2010 Haitian earthquake hit Haiti's capital city, Port-au-Prince, without warning. The effects in such a poor country, where people live crowded together in low-quality buildings, were terrible. Many buildings simply collapsed, leaving more than a million people homeless and more than 200,000 people dead.

Powerful Earthquakes

This table shows each year's most powerful earthquake since 2005.

Date	Location	Magnitude	Deaths
March 28, 2005	Sumatra, Indonesia	8.6	1,313
November 15, 2006	Kuril Islands, Russia	8.3	0
September 12, 2007	Sumatra, Indonesia	8.5	25
May 12, 2008	Sichuan, China	7.9	87,587
September 29, 2009	Samoan Islands	8.1	192
February 27, 2010	Maule, Chile	8.8	1

In January, 2010, the earthquake that struck Port-au-Prince, the capital of Haiti, did tremendous damage due to the city's high population.

WHAT CAUSES EARTHQUAKES?

Earthquakes happen when *tectonic plates* suddenly move. The speed and size of the plate movement determines how violent the earthquake will be.

Tectonic Plates and Fault Lines

Earthquakes happen where tectonic plates meet, and along cracks in the plates, called **fault lines**.

Plate Movement

Where tectonic plates meet, one of three things happens:
- one plate is forced below the other (a subduction fault)
- the plates slide past one another (a transform fault)
- the plates pull apart (a spreading zone).

Earthquakes usually happen on subduction or transform faults.

EYEWITNESS WORDS

G. A. Raymond witnessed the 1906 San Francisco, United States, earthquake:

"I looked up. The air was filled with falling stones. People around me were crushed to death on all sides. All around the huge buildings were shaking and waving. Every moment there were [noises] like 100 cannons going off at one time."

Two tectonic plates meet at the San Andreas Fault in California, United States. It is the site of many damaging earthquakes.

Fault Lines

Earthquakes happen along fault lines when one plate tries to move but another plate stays still or tries to move in the opposite direction. Tension builds up along the fault line and eventually the plate cannot stand the strain and snaps into a new position. This "snap" sends out waves of energy that shake the surface of Earth.

This diagram shows the key features of an earthquake.

The 2008 Nias Island Earthquake
Magnitude: 8.7
Date: March 28, 2005
Location: Nias Island, Indonesia

The 2008 Nias Island earthquake was so powerful that the shocks were felt in Bangkok, Thailand, more than 620 miles (1,000 km) away. It lasted two minutes and was followed by eight smaller quakes over the next 24 hours. More than 1,000 people died on Nias, and 300 more people died on other islands.

Seismic waves:
Waves of energy that spread out from the hypocenter

Hypocenter:
Spot below the surface where the earthquake begins

Epicenter:
Place on the surface above the hypocenter

Focal depth:
Distance from the surface to the epicenter

WHAT HAPPENS DURING AN EARTHQUAKE?

*Earthquakes do not always happen with just one **shock wave**. There can be a gap between shock waves of several minutes or several days. Once the quake begins, different types of shock waves act in different ways.*

Foreshocks, Main Shocks, and Aftershocks

Scientists divide earthquake shock waves into three categories, based on when they happen: **foreshocks**, main shock, and aftershocks.

Foreshocks

The first **tremors** people notice may be foreshocks. It only becomes clear that these tremors are actually foreshocks if they are followed by a more powerful earthquake.

Main Shock

The strongest shock wave is known as the main shock. This is the wave that records the highest score on the Richter scale for this set of shock waves.

Aftershocks

Aftershocks follow the main shock. There is no general rule about how powerful they will be. Sometimes the aftershock can be almost as strong as the main shock.

An earthquake's shock waves cause tremendous damage. In 1985, an earthquake struck Mexico City, causing buildings to collapse.

EYEWITNESS WORDS

Pablo Volenski experienced the 2010 Chilean earthquake:

"The north of Chile is a region where tremors are very common, so at the beginning I did nothing. But when … the walls started cracking, I took my sister in one arm and [ran] to the door."

After residents of Nias Island, off the coast of Sumatra, Indonesia, felt the shock waves of a massive earthquake, they fled buildings in search of safety.

Shock Waves

Scientists also divide shock waves into two types based on how the waves behave: body waves and surface waves.

Body Waves

Body waves travel through rock from the **epicenter** of an earthquake. There are two types of body wave, called primary waves and secondary waves. Primary waves travel at about 15,600 miles (25,200 km) per hour, and jiggle the rock backward and forward. Secondary waves travel at half the speed and lift the rock up and down.

Surface Waves

Surface waves travel along Earth's surface and are the most damaging earthquake waves. They are generated by body waves. The most damaging surface wave is a Rayleigh wave, which rolls along the ground like an ocean wave, at up to 745 miles (1,200 km) per hour. Damage is also caused by Love waves, which shake the ground from side to side.

DISASTER WORDS

epicenter place on Earth's surface directly above an earthquake

The 2010 Chilean Earthquake
Magnitude: 8.8
Date: February 27, 2010
Location: Maule region, Chile

Earthquakes regularly hit Chile, so when an earthquake hit in 2010, emergency plans were in place and people knew what to do. Partly as a result, relatively few people died. In Sumatra in 2005, a less powerful earthquake killed almost three times as many people.

WHAT HAPPENS AFTER AN EARTHQUAKE?

Once the main shock of an earthquake has finished, there are still plenty of physical dangers to watch out for, including mudslides, landslides, collapsing buildings, fires, and tsunamis.

DISASTER WORDS

liquefaction when soil turns from solid into a syrupy liquid

tremors earth-shaking movements

Mudslides and Landslides

Mudslides and landslides are common after earthquakes because of **liquefaction**, which happens when **tremors** shake soil that is full of water. Liquified ground can flow downhill, swallowing buildings and people in its path.

Collapsing Structures

Collapsing buildings, tunnels, and bridges are the main dangers during an earthquake. However, buildings can still fall down after the main shock has finished. Aftershocks make it more likely that buildings weakened by the main shock will collapse.

Following an earthquake, soil liquefaction can cause apartment buildings to lean or collapse.

EYEWITNESS WORDS

Iyvel Muresu witnessed the 2010 Haitian earthquake:

"We have been trying to save people, but the ground is still trembling. [Those trapped in collapsed buildings] have been asking for water and [are] hitting things to make noise, but we don't have the ability to save them."

This famous photo shows fire spreading rapidly through San Francisco after the 1906 earthquake.

Fires

Fires are a great danger to a city after an earthquake. In 1755, Lisbon, the capital of Portugal, was destroyed by fire after an earthquake. Collapsed wooden buildings were set alight by flames from stoves and lanterns. Today, damage to gas pipes and electrical cables can start fires after an earthquake.

Tsunamis

Powerful earthquakes under the ocean cause giant waves called tsunamis, which can cross an ocean very rapidly. When traveling they are usually 3 to 6 feet (1–2 m) high, but they slow down and grow much bigger as they approach land. A 32-foot (10-m) tsunami causes terrible destruction as it washes ashore.

The 1906 San Francisco Earthquake

Magnitude: 7.9 (estimated)
Date: April 18, 1906
Location: California, United States

Although the 1906 San Franciscan earthquake caused terrible damage, it was the fires that followed that had the worst effect. The fires burned for four days and destroyed more than 25,000 buildings. More than 3,000 people died and more than half the city's people were left homeless.

WHAT DAMAGE DO EARTHQUAKES CAUSE?

The damage that earthquakes cause depends on the strength of the earthquake and where it happens. Earthquakes kill and injure more people in densely populated areas.

Earthquake Intensity

The **magnitude** of an earthquake is measured on a scale called a Richter scale, which measures the shaking and gives an idea of how damaging the earthquake will be. The intensity of an earthquake depends on how close you are to its **epicenter**.

Human Impact

Earthquakes affect people by killing and injuring them, and by damaging property.

Killing and Injuring People

When an earthquake happens, people may be killed or injured by falling buildings, mudslides, landslides, fires, or tsunamis. People living in built-up areas such as cities are at the greatest risk.

Damaging Property

Earthquakes destroy homes and other buildings, leaving people with nowhere to live. After the 2010 Haitian earthquake, more than a million people were left homeless.

The Richter Scale

Number	Description	Effect	Per Year
up to 3.9	Micro/minor	May be felt, but rarely cause damage	300,000+
4–4.9	Light	Indoor items shake, minor damage only	6,200
5–5.9	Moderate	Major damage to badly built structures	800
6–6.9	Strong	Possible destruction spread over 50-mile (80-km) radius	120
7–7.9	Major	Serious damage over large areas	18
8–9.9	Great	Major damage over thousands of miles	1
10+	Epic	Massive destruction	0.5

Environmental Impact

Earthquakes affect the natural environment and the animals that depend on it for survival.

Damage to the Environment

The shock waves of a powerful earthquake can make trees sway so much that they snap. Whole areas of land can be buried under mudslides, and streams and rivers can alter their course. There is a danger that poisonous chemicals or **sewage** are released into the environment during an earthquake when containers and pipes break apart.

Animals and Earthquakes

Landslides and mudslides bury animals' homes, as well as their feeding or watering grounds. If rivers and streams change course, the fish, plants, and animals that rely on that water are affected.

DISASTER WORDS

sewage toilet waste from people's homes

evacuated helped to leave a dangerous place

PREDICTING EARTHQUAKES

Earthquakes cannot be accurately predicted. However, scientists are able to spot early-warning signs that an earthquake may be starting. To do this, they study a region's earthquake history and measure the level of tension building up along the fault line.

Earthquake History

Scientists use a region's earthquake history to help warn people when to expect the next earthquake.

History-Based Predictions

If there have been four extreme earthquakes in a specific area in the last 200 years, it is likely there will be another one in the next 50 years. If it has been more than 50 years since the last extreme earthquake, people often say that an earthquake is overdue.

Problems with Historical Predictions

Predictions based on historical data alone are not very accurate, because earthquakes often happen in groups rather than being evenly spaced out. When a fault line moves and causes an earthquake, it often puts added strain on another part of the fault line. This triggers another earthquake a few years later.

The San Francisco Bay Area experienced major earthquakes in 1838, 1868, 1906, and 1989. Another is predicted in the next few decades.

Fault-Line Tension

Scientists can estimate the amount of tension that builds up along fault lines, as parts of a tectonic plate strain to move against each another. As the tension increases, it becomes more likely that there will be an earthquake. If the scientists also know the level of tension before the last major earthquake, it makes their predictions more accurate. Unfortunately, this type of historical information is available for only a few of the world's fault lines.

California Earthquake Probability

The state of California, United States, has suffered many damaging earthquakes. In 2008, the United States Geological Survey investigated the region's earthquake history and current fault-line tension. They warned that there was a 99 percent likelihood of California experiencing at least one major earthquake in the next 30 years.

Magnitude	Likelihood in Next 30 Years, Northern California	Likelihood in Next 30 Years, Southern California
6.7	93 percent	97 percent
7	68 percent	82 percent
7.5	15 percent	37 percent
8	15 percent	3 percent

Tens of millions of people live near the San Andreas Fault in California, United States, and it is one of the most closely monitored fault lines in the world.

MONITORING EARTHQUAKES

By monitoring earthquakes from the moment the initial tremors are detected, it may be possible to warn people that an earthquake is on its way. The warning may be hours, minutes, or just a few seconds ahead of the main shock waves.

Measuring Seismic Activity

Seismic activity is measured using a seismometer, which records vibrations within Earth's crust and draws them on a chart called a seismogram.

Foreshock Warnings

Scientists start to monitor **foreshocks** hours or days before most major earthquakes occur, so local people can be warned. If minor earthquakes happen in areas where experts think a major earthquake could be about to happen, the authorities may warn people to **evacuate**.

Difficulties with Foreshock Warnings

The difficulty with using foreshocks as a prediction tool is that less than ten percent of minor earthquakes turn out to be foreshocks. The rest are just minor earthquakes. This means that there is the potential for many unnecessary evacuations.

A seismometer records vibrations by drawing a series of lines on a seismogram.

The seismometer draws a constant line.

Even tiny movements show up.

Large seismic movement is shown as high peaks.

In Japan, earthquake early-warning systems are able to stop the country's high-speed bullet trains as soon as a major earthquake is detected.

Early-Warning Systems

Japan, Mexico, and Taiwan monitor seismic activity as the first stage of their earthquake early-warning systems (EEWS). Other countries have more limited versions of these systems.

How EEWS Work

EEWS monitor the early stages of a major earthquake, then use high-speed computers to send out warning signals.

Amount of Warning Given

EEWS can provide up to 30 seconds' warning that an earthquake is happening. However, there might be less time after the warning. If the epicenter is nearby, the warning might even arrive after the shock waves.

Purposes of EEWS

With warning, trains and cars can stop moving, aircraft can be prevented from landing, and powerful machines can be shut down. If warnings are given to the general public, people may have enough time to reach a safer location.

The 2007 West Sumatran Earthquake

Magnitude: 6.4
Date: March 6, 2007
Location: Sumatra, Indonesia

The 2007 West Sumatran earthquake caused about 15,000 buildings to collapse, but killed relatively few people. The two significant foreshocks had warned people to leave buildings before the main shock caused the buildings to collapse.

BEFORE AN EARTHQUAKE STRIKES

How do the authorities deal with earthquakes? Earthquakes happen so quickly that plans and preparations must be made long before the earthquake actually strikes.

DISASTER WORDS

damper device to minimize movement

Taipei 101 stands 1,670 feet (509 m) high and is one of the world's tallest buildings. Special features stop it toppling over during an earthquake or high winds.

Preparing Buildings

Collapsing buildings are the biggest single cause of death in an earthquake. Governments can help prevent these deaths by making sure buildings and structures are designed to remain standing during an earthquake. Reinforced frameworks, extra-strong concrete and specially toughened building materials can all be used to make buildings, bridges, and tunnels stronger.

EYEWITNESS WORDS

David Wald of the United States Geological Survey emphasized the need for all buildings in earthquake zones to be strongly built:

"Earthquakes don't kill people, buildings kill people.'"

A **damper** hangs inside the top of the building to counteract any swaying movement.

20

Preparing People

It is important that people know how to act if an earthquake happens. In Japan, people may only get 30 seconds' warning that an earthquake is coming. This precious time will be wasted if they do not know the safest place to shelter. The Japanese government, like many others, asks all of its citizens to practice earthquake **drills**.

Preparing for the Aftermath

The authorities plan how they will help people after an earthquake happens. The police, hospitals, fire service, and armed forces all have plans for what they must do. They regularly practice so that things will go as smoothly as possible if an earthquake hits.

DISASTER WORDS

drills practices or rehearsals

The 2008 Sichuan Earthquake

Magnitude: 7.9
Date: May 12, 2008
Location: Sichuan, China

The 2008 earthquake in Sichuan, China, affected a huge area. Many buildings had been poorly built, and more than five million buildings collapsed. Dams and other structures also collapsed, and 87,587 people died. Lack of preparation made the death and destruction worse than it would otherwise have been.

During earthquake drills, Japanese schoolchildren wear padded hats and take shelter under reinforced desks.

ARE YOU AT RISK?

Are you and your family at risk from an earthquake? Your local library and council offices, and the Internet, are good places to start to investigate the area where you are living or staying.

The Modified Mercalli Intensity (MMI) Scale

The MMI scale is a way of describing how powerful an earthquake is on Earth's surface.

MMI Level	Description
I to III	May not be felt; if noticed, will feel similar to a passing truck.
IV to VI	Probably felt, but only slight effects (for example, heavy furniture moves).
VII to VIII	Specially designed buildings suffer slight damage; ordinary buildings significantly damaged.
IX to XI	Few structures survive.
XII	Complete destruction.

Key Questions

Measure the risk from an earthquake by asking key questions about an area's earthquake history, and whether there are preparations in place in case an earthquake happens. Ask the following questions about where you live, or where you are vacationing.

Has an Earthquake Happened Here Before?

Earthquakes happen regularly in areas where plates and fault lines are constantly building up tension. If earthquakes have hit on previous occasions, they are certain to happen again.

How Severe Was the Earthquake?

If an area has suffered from damaging earthquakes above level VI on the Modified Mercalli Intensity scale, you need to be prepared.

There have been many serious earthquakes throughout Japan's history. Traditional buildings are made of light, easily replaceable materials such as wood and paper.

How Old Is the Building You Are in?

Modern construction materials and techniques mean that newer buildings can be made stronger than older buildings. However, not all countries have the same building standards. After the 2009 L'Aquila earthquake in Italy, it was reported that even some modern buildings were poorly built, leading to an unnecessarily high **death toll**.

Are You in a Tall Building?

Tall buildings swing or sway more during an earthquake, so they need to be especially well built to avoid collapse. Remember – it takes a long time to leave a tall building if you are on one of the higher floors.

Older buildings in L'Aquila, Italy were built before engineers understood how to make buildings earthquake-proof.

The 2009 L'Aquila Earthquake

Magnitude: 5.8
Date: April 6, 2009
Location: Abruzzo, Italy

The Italian city of L'Aquila has been hit by at least eight earthquakes since 1315, and was destroyed by one in 1703. The city was rebuilt, so many city-center buildings dated from the 1700s. When an earthquake struck in 2009, large numbers of these buildings collapsed and more than 300 people died.

TOP TIPS FOR REDUCING RISK

While governments have emergency plans for earthquakes, it is also important to take responsibility for yourself. What can you do to reduce the risk to yourself and your family if an earthquake strikes?

Preparing an Emergency Plan

Your family plan says what everyone in the family should do if an earthquake strikes. Key things to include are:

- the safest places to shelter at home
- a safe place to meet once the earthquake is over
- the location of your family's emergency kit.

Know the Warning Signs

Make sure you are familiar with any warnings that might sound or be seen. These could be **foreshocks**, or they could be warnings on TV or radio.

Preparing an earthquake emergency kit of basic provisions and equipment will help to reduce the risk of injury to yourself or your family.

Earthquake Emergency Kit

Your emergency kit should include:
- enough food and water for several days (include food that will not spoil)
- a first-aid kit
- a charged mobile phone containing emergency phone numbers
- a wind-up radio and torch
- warm clothes.

It is believed that some animals, such as birds, can sense approaching earthquakes because they have more sensitive hearing than humans.

Earthquake Myths

There are lots of myths about earthquakes. Believing some of these could cost your life.

1 *There is a special type of "earthquake weather."*

  False! Earthquakes can happen in any kind of weather.

2 *An extreme earthquake will not strike where there have been lots of small strikes, because Earth has "let off steam."*

  False! The small strikes could be foreshocks.

3 *Earthquakes happen when the planets are in alignment, which exerts extra gravitational forces on Earth.*

  False! There is no connection.

4 *In an earthquake you might fall into a crack in Earth.*

  Technically possible! However, you are more likely to take up ice-skating and win an Olympic figure-skating gold medal a year later.

WHAT YOU CAN DO IF AN EARTHQUAKE HAPPENS

Once an earthquake has started, how should you react? Your chances of survival might depend on finding a safe location to wait out the earthquake. Your actions will depend on whether you are indoors, outside, or in a moving vehicle.

If You Are Indoors

If an earthquake starts when you are indoors:

- take shelter under a sturdy table or desk, or crouch in an inside corner of the building or a strongly supported, load-bearing doorway
- if in bed, stay there and protect your head with a pillow, unless you are under a heavy light fitting that could fall
- keep away from windows, outside walls, and anything that could fall on you
- stay where you are until the shaking has definitely stopped – many injuries happen when people try to move about too soon
- do not use elevators.

Wherever you are, practice looking for the safest places. That way, if disaster strikes you will automatically know where to shelter.

This Pakistani family was sleeping when an earthquake shook their home in October 2005.

Bridges such as this flyover in Los Angeles, California, United States, have been designed to break into sections during an earthquake.

If You Are Outdoors

Most earthquake casualties are caused by collapsing walls, flying glass, and falling objects. The safest places are away from buildings, streetlights, and power cables, in an open space such as parkland. You may have to crawl to get there! Once you reach an open space, stay there.

If You Are in a Vehicle

Stop the vehicle as quickly as possible and stay inside. Modern vehicles are designed to survive crashes. If possible, do not stop near or under buildings, trees, overpasses, or wires. Once the earthquake has stopped, avoid roads, bridges, or ramps that might have been damaged.

 EYEWITNESS WORDS

Tom Burt was caught outside in the 1964 Alaskan earthquake and tried to make it home:

"I must have fallen several times running home. The Earth was moving so much, you just couldn't keep your feet under you."

27

AFTER AN EARTHQUAKE

*The danger is not over when the ground stops shaking. The **aftermath** of an earthquake can be almost as dangerous as the earthquake itself. You may find yourself trapped under a collapsed building, or in desperate need of food, water, and shelter.*

After an earthquake struck the Sichuan province of China in May, 2008, the army helped injured survivors who had been trapped in the rubble.

If Trapped under Debris

The key dangers for anyone trapped under **debris** are fire, finding it hard to breathe, and not being rescued. Take the following precautions:

- Never light matches, in case leaking gas explodes.
- Do not move more than necessary: it will kick up dust and make it hard to breathe.
- Cover your mouth with clothing or a handkerchief.
- Tap on a pipe or wall to help the rescuers find you. Shouting may mean inhaling dangerous amounts of dust.

EYEWITNESS WORDS

Dorian Bell witnessed the aftermath of the 2009 earthquake in Padang, Indonesia:

"I wanted to spend the night in a hotel .... The biggest one was still standing, but it was closed. That was lucky, because that same hotel collapsed during the aftershock."

After the 2005 Kashmir earthquake, hundreds of thousands of people had to take shelter in tents.

If Free to Move about

During the aftermath, most earthquake survivors will have three key needs:
- getting medical care for injured people
- finding food, water, and shelter
- finding somewhere safe for their families and possessions.

Help arrives fastest in large towns and cities. However, overcrowding, disease, and crime can be problems in urban areas. If you are comfortable where you are, it might be best to stay there for a while. Wherever you are, it is important to stay calm, help other people, and work with the authorities.

The 2005 Kashmir Earthquake
Magnitude: 7.6
Date: October 8, 2005
Location: Azad Kashmir, Pakistan

The 2005 earthquake in Kashmir, Pakistan, killed almost 75,000 people and left up to three million people homeless. It happened just as the freezing winter began, and many survivors were forced to sleep outside in the cold.

29

QUIZ: DO YOU KNOW WHAT TO DO?

Now that you have read about earthquakes, do you feel you would have a better chance of survival? Test yourself using this quiz.

1 When is an earthquake most likely to happen?

a Earthquakes can happen at any time, day or night.
b On hot days.
c During rush hour, because the extra traffic causes disturbances.

2 If the ground starts to shake then stops again without causing any damage, what should you do?

a Wait in a secure spot until you feel certain no further **tremors** are coming.
b Immediately start tweeting your friends.
c Go outside and have a look around.

3 In an earthquake, what causes the most deaths?

a Falling buildings.
b People being swallowed by cracks in Earth that close over them, like in Hollywood movies.
c Car crashes.

4 Where is the best place to take cover during an earthquake?

a Under a desk or strong table, or an inside corner of the room.
b In open parkland.
c Both of the above.

5 What are you most likely to need once the earthquake has finished?

a Food and water to last until help arrives, plus somewhere warm and safe to sleep.
b A shower to wash off all that building dust.
c A camera to take some photos for the newspapers.

How did you do?

Mostly b or c answers: If you are planning on spending time in an earthquake zone, you had better read this book again. At the moment, you would be at risk of injury.

Mostly or all a answers: Not only would you have a good chance of survival, you might also be able to help other people stay safer during an earthquake.

DISASTER WORDS

tremors earth-shaking movements

DISASTER WATCHING ON THE WEB

Being on disaster watch means being prepared. It also means knowing where to get information ahead of a disaster, knowing how disasters happen, receiving disaster warnings, and getting updates on what is happening after a disaster has struck.

Find out More about Earthquakes

Check out these web sites to find out more about earthquakes.

- **www.howstuffworks.com**
  A search of this site for "earthquake" leads to information on how earthquakes happen, prediction methods, advice on how to survive an earthquake, a 'Fact or fiction?' earthquake quiz – and lots more!

- **www.weatherwizkids.com**
  Despite being a weather site, there is lots of information here about earthquakes, including an animated photo of a shaking city. There is also a link to an animation showing the different types of shock waves volcanoes cause (or go there direct: http://tinyurl.com/yzvlkxy).

- **http://news.google.com**
  Go to the search box and put in "earthquake," and Google News will take you to the most recent reports of earthquake activity around the world.

Earthquakes near you

Could an earthquake affect your local area, and what warning might you get? To find out, contact your local government and see whether:

- they have an earthquake emergency plan
- they know of a web site you can look at for warnings of seismic activity.

Your local library might also be able to help you find this information.

Alternatively, this web site should give you information about any major seismic activity in your area:

- **www.pdc.org** has a live map of current disasters (including earthquakes, volcanoes, floods, and extreme storms), which you can click on to find out more. There is also an excellent resources section, with information about earthquakes and other disasters.

INDEX